Marie MacCuish

Remembering Jerusalem

REMEMBERING JERUSALEM

POEMS BY

Rowan Williams

THE PERPETUA PRESS

OXFORD

The Perpetua Press
26 Norham Road, Oxford OX2 6SF

ISBN 1 870882 15 6

Printed in Great Britain by
Oxuniprint, Oxford University Press

CONTENTS

TRANSLATIONS

PREFACE

The bulk of this collection is contained in three clusters of poems (clusters rather than sequences, I think, as the order is not of major significance). The first began with a visit to Jerusalem during Orthodox Holy Week in 1995, and makes a fair amount of allusion to the sites and ceremonies of the season; Abu Ghosh is one of the sites traditionally (though not very plausibly) identified with the Emmaus of St Luke's Gospel, scene of the resurrected Jesus's self-disclosure at the end of a journey, when he is recognised as he silently breaks bread. Today, Abu Ghosh is the location of a Benedictine community of French origin.

The 'Graves and Gates' poems reflect a period of several years marked by the death of parents and some close friends, among them the extraordinary figure of Gillian Rose, Jewish philosopher and critic, baptised on the day of her death. Around all this, I found myself thinking about death in general, and about the deaths of some of those I love and admire from a distance as persons and writers; exploring how their deaths uncannily 'metaphorise' something central to their work and thought (Simone Weil's apparent self-starvation, Rilke's throat cancer . . .).

'Celtia' embodies a lasting scepticism about some modern romantic pictures of Celtic identity, looking instead at bits of the ancient Celtic world, in the literal form of artefacts from that age and also in the shape of fragments from one or two of the classical writers who describe it.

As in my earlier collection, *After Silent Centuries*, there are some free translations: three from fairly well-known Rilke poems ('Todes-Erfahrung', 'Das Karusell' and 'Der Engel', the originals in *Neue Gedichte/New Poems*, translated by Stephen Cohn, Manchester, Carcanet, 1997, pp. 83, 101 and 67 respectively), one from the Welsh of Waldo Williams—'Mewn Dau Gae', *Dail Pren*, Llandysul, Gomer, new edition 1991, pp. 25–6, one of the foremost works of twentieth-century Welsh poetry, and probably Waldo's finest poem.

As to the other poems, it helps to know that in 1966 Thomas Merton, the radical monastic genius, poet and social critic, was entangled in a tormenting and unconsummated love affair; and that Penrhys is a council estate in the Rhondda Valley, and also (like Walsingham) the site of a medieval shrine of Our Lady.

ROWAN WILLIAMS

First Thing

The last bit of the dream is letters falling,
soft and regular, the papery flutter
rhythmic on the mat. Not unlike
grey tides licking sand. Waking
is water leaking in; the stuff
out there wobbles and swells
and settles grudgingly into a dryish
daytime shape. And the letters
leaking in resolve themselves
as the dry short breaths
of a nextdoor body, finding
its way out of the night
into slow breakfast time,
the food, the light, a few words,
and the apprehensive, unavoidable
opening of envelopes.

Dream

News of another ceasefire broken: Sarajevo?
somewhere like that. Anger and shame. I stammer
to the person I am drinking with and who I don't
know very well. I'm crying, quite a lot (I do
in dreams). We are due, next, at a seminar
on violence, held in a courthouse or a theatre,
something like that. What I remember is two speakers,
one cropped and harsh: I find it hard
to formulate my question. One bearded,
articulate and reasonable, talking of victims,
tragedy, the pathos of God trapped in a world
of risks. He sounds like dense stringed music.
It is time to leave, and I fall into step
with him or someone from the benches opposite
(theatre? chapel? parliament?), bearded,
articulate and friendly. We have much in common.
He leads me round behind the theatre
or courthouse; the path narrows between iron railings.
He rounds a corner. There is no one. Stone and iron
closing in. In front of me , a haze of wasps,
alive and dead, some sticking in the dense
and whiteish webbing stuck across the path. I feel
my legs slow down; I know there is no corner
left to turn. I feel the first sting on my right hand
between wrist and thumb. I know I am going to die.

Feofan Grek: the Novgorod Frescoes

Did Yeats mean this?[1] because when sages
stand in the fire, this happens. Skin
umbers and cracks and shines. And then
on hands, shoulders and skirts, the splash
and dribble; you could think the bells have melted from their perch,
so that the roaring hollows fall, lazy as snow,
bright liquid pebbles. And then, long
after the eyes have gone, the cheekbones
gleam, razored with little scars in parallel,
the surgery of initiation, letting through
furnaces under the dun hard skin.
We slow down more and more as the heat rises; surfaces
dry up, something inside swells painfully.
The razor makes its first cut. From the oven walls,
out of the searing dusk, they smile
(not at us) blindly.

[1] In his poem 'Sailing to Byzantium'.

Thomas Merton: Summer 1966

Bright post-examination weather; in the redundant
classroom, the only point seems here, the belly
of Kentucky heat, the shaven sweating mariners
singing Gregorian shanties in a slow
light evening. What do I want? What sixteen-year-olds want,
no doubt; but also: to learn how to sail that sweaty ship,
words falling moistly from the timber, shining,
Latin, American, French. And the horizon that you think
(so slow the light, so slow the gestures and the voices)
night never quite closes on.

                    The same month
you made a landfall, emptied on to the shore,
gasping and heaving against a new hard element,
against the solid sand. And now I read you, years on,
leap and flail, mouth wide, reaching—you once-fluent fellow—
for the words to fix it, finding in the unfixable
a bizarre homeliness. You spent my sixteenth birthday
making a clean(ish) breast of things to the steel smile
of Abbot James. You staged show after show
for friends, then cancelled. Not to make sense is
what most matters.

                  What was I seeing,
then, that summer? light from a dead star?
Not quite. But who could tell the night, closing its mouth,
the hard sand, were, after all, where the hot songs
would lead? Practise the Gothic scales for long enough
and they will conjure, surprisingly, this place, flat concrete blocks,
convenience foods, an empty page to look into,
finding the anger; painting, then blotting faces you might wear,
hers, yours, that only in fiction would stand still.
Not to make sense. inside the keel of sweating ribs,
not to make sense but room.

Walsingham: the Holy House

Red kites against a dark blue sky: the flames
beating and clapping round their poise, they fight
wordlessly to hold upright against the draught.

The fat nightlights grow steep, briefly
narrowing their upended eyes, the wavering lines
converge, drop like a plumb, and for a moment

Breath sits upright against the draught, the fat flesh
caught where the beams cross, soundless, perhaps
frightened: fast, without strain, the fire stoops.

Penrhys

The ground falls sharply; into the broken glass,
into the wasted mines, and turds are floating
in the well. Refuse.

May; but the wet, slapping wind is native here,
not fond of holidays. A dour council cleaner,
it lifts discarded

Cartons and condoms and a few stray sheets
of newspaper that the wind sticks
across his face—

The worn sub-Gothic infant, hanging awkwardly
around, glued to a thin mother.
Angelus Novus:

Backing into the granite future, wings spread,
head shaking at the recorded day,
no, he says, refuse,

Not here. Still, the wind drops sharply.
Thin teenage mothers by the bus stop
shake wet hair,

Light cigarettes. One day my bus will come, says one;
they laugh. More use 'n a bloody prince,
says someone else.

The news slips to the ground, the stone dries off,
smoke and steam drift uphill
and tentatively

Finger the leisure centre's tense walls and stairs.
The babies cry under the sun,
they and the thin girls

Comparing notes, silently, on shared
unwritten stories of the bloody stubbornness
of getting someone born.

Curtains for Bosnia

Not iron but glass; smoother, bewildering.
We couldn't understand why they
Would shake their heads and shrug,
Not understanding, when they looked so near.

And not a curtain but a dome:
Rays from a reasonable sun drawn in ,
Bent into thick and beaming probes, to drive
Rational passions deep into the soil,

Where the roots swelled, grew muscular
Grew dense and anxious in the dark,
Began to feel out for a grip to choke
Each other, sent up damp and glaring shoots.

Inexorable soft pressures crack the glass.
Cold; other sounds; then piece by piece,
the shards drop a sky's worth of reasonable light
Slicing the crowded greenery.

Who knows where the sky's needles go,
Whose flesh is cut? But the ground dries,
Under the sun, and the fat roots grow spindly
As old limbs do when there's no more blood to spare.

The devil, said the witches, had an iron prick,
Icecold and smooth. Glass into iron; a reasonable sun,
Nourishing, resolving, folds into a shaft
Of rapists' surgery, till there's no more blood to spare.

So much, we say, for warm and clear illusion,
For the sealed surfaces of thought that incubate
The vegetable nightmares, fright, despair.
Now they can hear the music of our ironies.

Only: now we can hear, wishing
We couldn't understand, they look so near.

REMEMBERING JERUSALEM

Jerusalem Limestone

I

When you try
to cultivate a plot by the Dead Sea,
you find that pouring on fresh water
brings the salt
nearer the surface.

Up on the hills,
the lurching terraces are full of vines
and olives, and the terraces are rimmed
with stone, white
as a scrubbed doorstep,

White as the scurf
meandering the length of a cold shore
after polluted tides, as if the oil
and wine drained
down at last

Into a thirst
of sand and sea-water, a mouth
at the far edge of words or breath, a face
with salt
breaking the surface

II

And when you see
the staircase hills, white, olive, grey,
the stones hang there like snow
along the edge
of evergreens.

The vines and groves
are posies, stuck by children's hands

into the winter soil, hard
under blankets;
tomorrow dead.

Winter's what lasts.
The oil glow sinking like bonfires
into grey flakes, a twisted log
or two, already
slipping down

Under tonight's
fresh fall; only the cold
can be relied on to come back.
The wine is chilled
long before harvest.

III

When you touch,
your hands will come away dry,
faintly powdered, classroom hands, to rub
back into damp
adhesive life

Up on the hills
the lurching lines cover the board
we can't decode. This is a country
thick with scripts
most won't know.

But the dust
sits in the folds of clothes
and lungs and larynx. What we want
to say explodes,
a chalky retching.

Winter.
the dusty coughs like guns,
The class dismissed, untaught.
Something not understood.
The white dry hill.

Gethsemane

Who said that trees grow easily
compared with us? What if the bright
bare load that pushes down on them
insisted that they spread and bowed
and pleated back on themselves and cracked
and hunched? Light dropping like a palm
levelling the ground, backwards and forwards?

Across the valley are the other witnesses
of two millennia, the broad stones
packed by the hand of God, bristling
with little messages to fill the cracks.
As the light falls and flattens what grows
on these hills, the fault lines dart and spread,
there is room to say something, quick and tight.

Into the trees' clefts, then, do we push
our folded words, thick as thumbs?
somewhere inside the ancient bark, a voice
has been before us, pushed the densest word
of all, abba, and left it to be collected by
whoever happens to be passing, bent down
the same way by the hot unreadable palms.

Calvary

The metalled O. Like Bethlehem, like
a baroque drain in the marble floor;
when your hand has been sucked in, it comes away
from its complicity moist,
grimy, sweet-scented.

The Stone of Anointing

All day they oil and polish, rubbing
as if the stone were troubled, rippled with
the angel's windy touch; as if the stone
were sprung like a cramped muscle, and a hard warm hand
could loosen it; as if the hoarse determined breath
and the hot oil could stop the choking, break a seal
on some unseen and frozen lung.
As if they couldn't see themselves. And only when
the stone falls still will their tired polished
faces look back at them; ready to receive
Christ laid on them like a cloth.

Easter Eve: Sepulchre

Constantine knew, of course, just what he wanted:
smooth verticals and marble, crushed glass rolled underfoot,
room for archangels with their orbs and wands,
space for cool power to stroll, relaxed and heavy-footed

Out to the little scented hedges, under a cross that shimmers,
silver and rubies, soft shadows lapping at the ankles.
He cut and smoothed, levelled and piled and spread:
light; crystal; breezy veils; a new, enlightened holy hill.

History (or something) disagreed. The centuries squared up,
exchanged curt, recognizing nods, moved in,
folded and packed, crumpled and stripped and boxed:
the shadows shook themselves, lurched up and smiled

From a new height; people found other things
to do with silver. Air from the marble lungs
is punched out, and the colonnades are crushed and processed
into a maze of ditches, damp stone capsules,

Whorls, cavities, corners with don't-ask smells
and fairground decoration. A collapsing star, screwing its stuff
into the dark: soaring heat, density, a funnel
spinning towards the opposite of anything.

* * *

Saturday afternoon, the bodies squashed, wet, boxed,
breathing into the shadows full of smells and tinsel;
flame leaks and spits out of the singularity,
sparks a cracked bell. Iron, rope, smoke

Pant in the tight dark, a light-footed,
high-strung passing. Afterwards we breathe,
dry off the sweat and crying, ask what history
is after, bullying us into waking, into this oppositeness.

Low Sunday: Abu Ghosh

Calm, fluent, the Mass moves
like robes on a walking body, upright
and in no hurry, the chanted French
swings loose between the stresses.

Finding its way in here
something not quite the hard dawn,
crackling out of the grave, but
heavy, lumbering maybe, quiet,

As it pads in from downstairs,
lies down and looks at us, something
idle (maybe), breathing just audibly,
not without noticing; not to be avoided.

GRAVES AND GATES

'. . . that through the grave and gate of death we may pass to our joyful resurrection'

BOOK OF COMMON PRAYER

Rilke's Last Elegy

Die ewige Strömung
          reisse durch beide Bereiche alle Alter
          immer mit sich und übertönt sie in beiden

The river flows in both kingdoms. On the side
we don't see, the moon side, it collects the things
we don't see: slivers of ice between the ripples,
and small blue leprosies, and tiny stars that prick
and cut us as we drink; moon-sounds, the anxious hawking
of a fox, the little screams of casual prey, the car-alarm
five silent streets away (you know that if you wake
and look, you'll never find it; it is another kingdom).

So when you whisper into the stream, the words run
round through the moon's valleys, where we don't see,
coming back strange: swollen or scarred, not lining up
and answering. This time round, they prick and scratch
the throat till it flows black, a winter river
fed by the rains we don't see. Bit by bit
the other kingdom spreads, and what we say drowns softly
all sounds smothered. Then the river dries. The earth

Puckers and shrinks, as quiet as the moon. And a few words
lie in their white bed, covenanting stones.

Nietzsche: Twilight

At the clinic, he broke windows, shouting
that there were guns behind them, desperate
not to be shielded by the thin, deceiving skin
that looked as if it wasn't there. He liked
the opaque curtain or the open sky; not this.
His mother took him home; out for walks,
she told him, Put on your nice professor's face,
when they met friends. His head grew vast,
pulling him downwards till he could not breathe.
At night he roared; during the day, My voice
is not nice, he would whisper. White,
swollen, his skull drowned him like a stone,
his breath, at the end, the sound
of footsteps on broken glass.

Simone Weil at Ashford

Upstairs into the air: a young god,
pupils dilated, blows into his little flute.
At each stair's end, he breaks it, reaches for a new one,
climbs again. Below the crowd blurs, hums,
ahead the sky is even, dark from the bare sun.
Breaking the last instrument, he waits,
and in a while they will tear out his heart,
now it is still and simple as the rise and fall
of tides. The crowd and the sun breathe him in.

No, we don't walk like him. We stagger up
the steps in padded jackets, moonboots,
crash-helmets, filters and shades. In gravity.
Some of us try to strip; but what's beneath
is very cold, even under the dark bare sun:
a stiff, gaunt crying, I must not be loved,
and I must not be seen, and if I cannot walk like god,
at least I can be light and hungry, hollowing my guts
till I'm a bone the sentenced god can whistle through.

Tolstoy at Astapovo[1]

Off through the looking-glass he ran:
into the world of hedges, brooks, black and white cantonments,
the snapping Queen to urge him on, the fevers
rising and falling, painting black or white
the country of his choices. All around the iron lines
run to a point. Ahead of him strolls Platon,
not looking back; he runs till he is breathless,
burning, but he can't catch him. In the next-door squares
the pieces crowd, the journalists, the relatives, the hopefuls,
the *starets* in the ladies' loo, the script consultants,
newsreel men, police. Check.

Heat and smoke in the little squares; shivering,
he thinks of taking up a long-lost country skill
as quaint as thatching, complicated, unselfconscious,
the sort of thing you pick up in the hours
of glazed winter boredom, the absent-minded endlessness
of a poor childhood. *How do peasants die?*
Some things you can't get into at this age. He knew
he was too old to die, fingers too stiff for plaiting
the spiny ends. He put his head down in the straw.
Mate. All the words came tumbling
backwards out of his dream.

[1] Leo Tolstoy died in the stationmaster's house (now a museum) in Astapovo
(now Tolstoy)

Winterreise: for Gillian Rose, 9 December 1995

Morning

The flat fields tramp towards the Severn.
I know there is no cliff to drop from
at their edge, only the sand and the wet still sheets.

This morning, though, the thick and chest-constricting
light, the level, rose-grey clouds and the remains
of icy fog stand between fields and water,

And the horizon has to be a steep edge, has to be
the cliff where Gloucester fell that never-to-be measured
drop from his body to the ground.

And down, a long way down, below the frost,
must be soft embers sending up the light
from fires the night-fog has muffled but not killed.

Afternoon

Still, where you were concerned, we always
arrived too late; too late, myopic, short of sleep,
with fingers stumbling to decipher messages
you left for us, engraved in a hard surface.
It was a distant relative of yours who drove
his lawyer's reed into the black Sinai basalt
till the calligraphy of little streams broke out
to age the hopeless rock as if with history,
as if with words; another kinsman, distant or not too distant,
writing in falling sweat on stone, body to ground, something
his friends never quite managed to read. Tracing, unthinkingly,
a pattern of spilled wine on the dayroom table,
never quite managing to meet each other's eyes, or not for long,
we test the feel of an unyielding difficulty, not yet sure
of handling this, of finding where the streams combine,
reading what the wet fingertips decode.

Night

Dying by degrees, perhaps, is a winter journey:
connections cancelled unexplained, the staff,
their patience ebbing, closing amenities, one by one, around you.

The temperature falls, and for an hour you sit
on a plastic bench, aching for sleep,
under the surly light that strips you

For some always-delayed inspection; so even,
so hard, that for so long you cannot see the dark;
the homely dark, with its fierce small fires.

Flight Path

For Delphine Williams; August 1999

Dead souls walk straight as Roman legions
from Bredon Hill, striding from fort to fort,
from one sullen, round-shouldered rise
to the next, stopping (perhaps) on each to gape
and swallow and exchange dumb looks, and wait for orders.

The track runs through the solid tribal world:
crosses a motorway at thirty seven degrees, lays
a cold strip across a sheep's back, slips
between cup and lip, between eye and screen, between
my child's hand and my own, eases between the window and the wind.

The Roman road ignores the aboriginals, their maps
and calendars. But we shuffling primitives can't fail to see
this is the occupying power. Sooner or later, we shall have to learn
to shape our mouths, measure our stride like theirs,
and look nowhere but to the next grazed, wind-scrubbed summit.

Ceibr: Cliffs

For Aneurin Williams; September 1999

The quilt of willowherb muffles
the stream before it drops
invisible to the beach;
the moist whisper thinned
in its straight seaward fall,
the shore sound coming back up, dry
as two palms rubbing steadily
close to your ear, or pages
fingered through, or a hand
stroking an unshaved cheek, hard;
or a thick old fabric, tearing
very slowly. Sea on stone
never settles for good if this
is a story of meeting or
an endless creeping scission:
a palmer's kiss, book skimmed
for the familiar quote, touching
the distant face against
hospital pillows, or
slow surgery, faded cloth
pulled and surrendering
every breath unstitching
something. Whatever,
the hoarse bass echo
doesn't change: just the one
voice, touching or tearing.

Windsor Road Chapel

Cinema (Odeon or Capitol) circa 1959:
only no curtains, just an even, tight-pinned bedsheet
of timber, and a blunt, empty cockpit.
Nothing, it says, will come over your shoulder,
no hidden reels, throwing a hazy line

Across the smoke to play the rainbow fish
that slip around, behind, our watered eyes.
This is the board for unexpected news,
a death, a resignation, raw, cold
as the air outside, flat as the turned-down wish.

God, it seems doesn't live in water, glimpse and flash,
mirror and shade, not still until the day's
damp end. The message on the wires
rubs at the skin's impatient folds
in dry, pale itches, drifts of my neighbour's ash.

The most familiar artefact of brass and pine
nags at the memory; you know what's going to fit
the timber cabinet before too long, the drought
that cures the flesh and seals the blood.
Board: gate: departure, says the sign.

Off you go , then, on static-laden floors,
drawn—as we all are —by unwelcome news;
but even now, not able not to pause
and listen for pursuing streams, rolled
shining and stuttering downhill to the exit doors.

CELTIA

Gundestrup: The Horned God

You know him. Sitting and sitting,
sitting until the moss grows
over his eyes, until

The stark bone branches
burst through his skull, until
his mouth and hand and gut will

Shape the one round, tense
metal syllable, at which
the beasts stand still

Snouts cocked and hairs on end,
the salmon frozen in mid-leap,
gripped by the unexpected rider's will.

Sit: till you grow hollow,
round as a cauldron, and your mouth
holds the world cocked, dumb and chill,

And from your brow the knitting bones
twist to a forest of hard sounds; among them things
stand still and frightened. Well

You know.

The Sky Falling

'They [the Celtic chiefs] told him that they feared
only one thing, that the sky should fall'

Arrian, *The Expedition of Alexander*

A joke, perhaps? They still
do it, solemnly meeting
the earnest foreigner's enquiry.
Because there could have been,
surely, no terror

For the lime-rinsed and technicolour-
shirted, head-hungry, henpecked
louts who so irritated
dry Caesar in the promise of an end
so brisk and flat

And messy, like flies squashed
between the pages as the book
claps shut; dying of the applause
of heaven and earth when they
join hands

At the show's end. Or maybe,
after all, serious. Think of them
lurching out of the doorway
to breathe, pee, vomit,
packed with booze

Kebabs and mutual admiration,
into the cold; the snow just starting
and the sky slips gently
and piecemeal into the grass
and vanishes,

Fragments of brief intricacy,
like the bard's lovely, hot,
cosseting songs indoors,
the words that freeze great doings
(rapes, wars)

In symmetries and stars; and going
nowhere. The stories sink
into the grass at night.
and the earth sits there,
not applauding,

Spreading an empty palm;
swallowing the sparks of damp
and formal brilliance. Very
quiet.
No joke.

Posidonius and the Druid

Ridges of bone, moulded, you'd think, by awkward thumbs,
freckles, red stubble, and the large pale astigmatic eyes;
the voice hoarse, fluent, not deep.
Well. People come, like you, he says, looking for secrets.
What we learned from Pythagoras. For a consoling echo
of your sweet doctrine from the untouched caves
of us poor primitives. (Leaning to me.) Do you like
what I've to show you? On his open hand
a knife, bone-handled, stained and smooth.
Your logos is a child, he says, chattering to itself
while it plays on the sand. I am a swimmer.
I am a salmon and a seal. My streams
are made of many fluids, dark swaying planes
on which I travel still as sleep; or where
I leap like silver. The sea. Rain on the skin,
and sweat. Tears and the river over stones.
My blood and yours: the tide that beats below the skin
or in the pulsing from the severed vein,
or from my organ, or from yours, or else the urine
from the hanged man, jerking among the leaves,
whose motions speak to me. Over these waves
I learn to skim my hands, and in these wells
my tongue explores, drinks words.

                         I take the knife;
like rubbing fingers on a worn inscription,
read it. In my mind, briefly: flat plains,
a straight road running to the edge of things, drab
unfamiliar carts packed close with silent people,
knowing and not knowing what this journey is
on which they're sent by blood and wisdom and
dark quiet waters, and I reach out breathless for the shore,
children and sand, the noise and the unsafety,
drift, spars and groundlessness, but still the anchorage
proper to talking beings.

Altar to the Mothers

Soft -cheeked and honey-breasted,
fruit tumbling at their feet like children, and
semantically-loaded sheaves of corn,
beautiful, terrible; warm thighs and mysteries
and a calm dark regard out of their timeless eyes . . .

Actually no (if this is really them):
they stand in solid sexless line,
headscarved and overcoated, waiting for a bus
to Ebbw Vale or Rotherham; bleak damp endurance of
the never-up-to-standard world.

Men (rightly) shivering laid oil and wine
and sacrificed new shoes, pubertal hair,
unsatisfactory girlfriends, self-respect,
nodding in desperation at the granite words
you can't switch off. No, you do what *you* want, love,

Don't think of me. We've always done what seemed the right thing
for you, pet. If you don't respect
yourself, no-one will do it for you. If you've got
your health, there's nothing you can't cope with. What time
do you call this? Why aren't you eating?

You do what you want, love. Divinity is manifest
in the sublime command. Ignore this order; making sure
that you won't, ever. Refused, victorious, inexpugnable,
they settle back, having secured that there will never be
an up-to-standard offering, a world

Free to leave home, to call time what we like.

TRANSLATIONS

Experiencing Death

Don't know a thing about this trip we're going on; they don't
give much away about it. So we don't know where to stand
to look at the unwelcome destination, how to see our death.
Amazed? entranced? or loathing? How the tragic mask twists things

Out of an honest shape! But still, the world can give
you quite a cast-list to choose from. Just don't
forget; as long as it's the audience's reaction
that worries you, death's at your elbow on the boards.

No audience fancies corpses. Only when *you* went offstage,
the flats you slipped through let in something else,
a streak of truth: the colour of real foliage
under real sunshine in a real woodland.

For us, the show must go on. All those lies
we learned, struggling and panicky, the stagey gestures
ordered by some director we can't put a face to . . . and then you,
struck off the list, you who are real now a long way off,

Your far-off thereness sometimes overtakes us still, falling
around us like that streak of daylight green, and then
we find, just for a bit, we can play life, not scripts;
not give a damn about applause.

(Rilke)

Roundabout, Jardin du Luxembourg

Out of that foreign land, the gaudy horses
bounce with conviction for a while (never mind
the shadows from the canopy) — the foreign land
that hangs around long enough after closing time before it fades.

They all look feisty enough, even the ones
(quite a few) with carts hitched on. Oh look!
A big bad lion seems to have got in. Oh look!
A sweet baby white elephant. What next?

Oh look! A stag, just like the ones you see
out in the woods, except of course this one
happens to have a little girl in blue
strapped in a saddle,

                    and the big bad lion's
carrying a little boy in white, who's hanging on
for dear life, while the lion grins and slobbers—
Look! the sweet baby white elephant again . . .

Those girls are getting too big for the ride,
but there they go, giggling and darting sparky looks
all over the place in mid-flight, and they—oh,
there's the sweet
               baby
                   white . . .

Round and round and round and round and round.
Red. Green. Grey. Red. Aching to stop.
Nowhere to go. The little profiles sketchy, hardly started.
Listen! There's someone laughing as they spin,
as if they were —well, happy, blissful even;
wasting their breath, casting a shimmer round
this blind asthmatic game.

                             (Rilke)

48

Angel

He bends his head away, says his hard No to everything
that might commit him, tie him down,
because there's always something circling, always
just about to land, something enormous
pushing up through his heart.

                    And the deep blackness
of the sky is full, for him, of shapes,
and any one of them could summon him—come here!
see this! So for God's sake, don't try to put
what weighs *you* down into those airy hands of his;
because it's you they'd grab for.

                    In the middle of the night
they'd burrow in and scrabble like a maniac
round your house, and clutch you, wrestle you to the floor,
squeezing and kneading, wanting to sculpt and hollow,
to push you, break you out of the form you know
                       that clothes you round.

                                (Rilke)

Between Two Fields

These two fields a green sea-shore, the tide spilling
radiance across them, and who knows
where such waters rise? And I'd had years
in a dark land, looking: where did it, where did he
come from then? Only he'd been there
all along. Who though? who
was this marksman loosing off bolts
of sudden light? One and the same the lightning
hunter across the field, the hand to tilt
and spill the sea, who from the vaults
above the bright-voiced whistlers, the keen darting plovers,
brought down on me such quiet, such

Quiet: enough to rouse me. Up to that day
nothing had worked but the hot sun to get me going,
stir up drowsy warm verses: like blossom
on gorse that crackles in the ditches, or
like the army of dozy rushes, dreaming
of clear summer sky. But now: imagination
shakes off the night. Someone is shouting
(who?), Stand up and walk. Dance. Look.
Here is the world entire. And in the middle
of all the words, who is hiding? Like this
is how it was. There on the shores of light
between these fields, under these clouds.

Clouds: big clouds, pilgrims, refugees,
red with the evening sun of a November storm.
Down where the fields divide, and ash and maple
cluster, the wind's sound, the sound of the deep,
is an abyss of silence. So who was it stood
there in the middle of this shameless glory, who
stood holding it all? Of every witness witness,
the memory of every memory, the life
of every life? who with a quiet word

calms the red storms of self, till all
the labours of the whole wide world
fold up into this silence.

And on the silent sea-floor of these fields,
his people stroll. Somewhere between them,
through them, around them, there is a new voice
rising and spilling from its hiding place
to hold them, a new voice, call it the poet's
as it was for some of us, the little group
who'd been all day mounting assault
against the harvest with our forks, dragging
the roof-thatch over the heavy meadow. So near,
we came so near then to each other, the quiet huntsman
spreading his net around us.
Listen! you can
just catch his whistling, hear it?

Whistling, across the centuries of blood
on the grass, and the hard light of pain; whistling
only your heart hears. Who was it then, for God's sake?
mocking our boasts, tracking our every trail and slipping past
all our recruiting sergeants? Don't you know?
says the whistling, Don't you remember?
don't you recognise? it says; until we do.
And then, our ice age over, think of the force
of hearts released, springing together, think
of the fountains breaking out, reaching up
after the sky, and falling back, showers
of falling leaves, waters of autumn.

Think every day, under the sun,
under these clouds, think every night of this,
with every cell of your mind's branching swelling shoots;
but with the quiet, the same quiet, the steady breath,
the steady gaze across the two fields, holding still
the vision: fair fields full of folk;

for it will come, dawn of his longed-for coming,
and what a dawn to long for. He will arrive, the outlaw,
the huntsman, the lost heir making good his claim
to no-man's land. the exiled king
is coming home one day; the rushes sweep aside
to let him through.

After the Welsh of Waldo Williams